LIVING HISTORY

THE VICTORIANS

Miriam Moss

Illustrated by Gerry Wood

Living History

The American West	The Middle Ages
The Ancient Britons	The Normans
Ancient China	North American
The Aztecs	Indians
Cavaliers and	The Romans
Roundheads	The Saxons
The Crusades	The Stuarts
The Egyptians	The Tudors
Great Explorers	The Victorians
The Greeks	The Vikings
The Incas	

First published in 1986 by
Wayland (Publishers) Ltd
61 Western Road, Hove,
East Sussex BN3 1JD, England

© Copyright 1986
Wayland (Publishers) Ltd

Phototypeset by
Kalligraphics Ltd, Redhill, Surrey
Printed and bound in Belgium by
Casterman S.A.

**British Library Cataloguing in
Publication Data**
Moss, Miriam
    The Victorians. – (Living history)
    1. Great Britain – Social life and
    customs – 19th century – Juvenile
    literature
    I. Title   II. Series
    941.081   DA533

ISBN 0–85078–808–0

All the words in the text which
appear in **bold** are explained in
the glossary on page 29.

Contents

The Victorian Age

Queen Victoria reigned from 1837 to 1901. During her reign there were many important changes. Industrial towns continued to grow and the new steam trains rattled across the countryside.

Laws were passed to improve people's lives. Working men were allowed to **vote**. Children were stopped from working long hours in terrible conditions and went to school for the first time. Goods poured from British factories to be sold all over the world. Britain had never been so rich. But at the end of Victoria's reign many people were still very poor.

Family life

The rich Victorians lived in beautiful homes with all the latest **inventions** like telephones and electricity. They wore fine clothes and had many servants, like the kitchen staff shown below. Manners were very important. Children were looked after by nannies and rarely saw their parents except at mealtimes.

Sunday was a day of rest, when families and their servants went to church. Sports were forbidden and all shops were closed. The rich ate large amounts of meat but the poor were often hungry. They lived in cramped, dark houses. Everyone in the family had to work to stay alive. They could not afford new clothes or toys.

Country life

Until about 1850 most people lived in the countryside. Country people worked as **blacksmiths**, carpenters, shepherds, saddlers and shoemakers. Wives worked in the dairy and children weeded or scared away the birds! Some farm workers were given cottages with their jobs. But these were often damp and unhealthy especially in winter.

Poor harvests and new machinery, like
this steam engine and **threshing machine**,
meant that there was less work on the
farms. So farm workers were often forced
to find factory work in the towns.

City life

Cities were very crowded. Workers lived in rows of houses built back to back in narrow alleys. The filthy streets caused outbreaks of disease, especially **cholera**. But in 1865 **sewers** were built and rubbish was removed.

City streets were full of boys who had run away from home to look for a job. They were called street arabs. They slept in doorways and begged or stole food. Some found jobs shining shoes or selling flowers. Many poor people were forced into a life of crime to stay alive. Most cities were badly lit and Britain's new police force had problems trying to keep law and order.

Working hard

Many Victorian families worked long hours and were very badly paid. A girl working in a brick factory had to move 36 tonnes of bricks in one day. Small boys climbed inside chimneys to clean them and children worked down coal mines pulling trucks through narrow tunnels. Many people were killed in the factories because the machines were so dangerous.

In the 1820s factory workers joined together to form unions. They refused to work until the **government** and the employers changed their working conditions. As a result, new laws were passed. Boys under twelve and women and girls were no longer allowed down coal mines. Dangerous machinery was fenced off.

Having fun

A rich family would entertain themselves by singing around a piano or reading stories and poems out loud. They sometimes went to a theatre or a concert. Poor children played in the dirty alleys where they might hear the mill worker's brass band or the miner's choir practising. They could also enjoy travelling fairs and circuses, and street entertainers like the **organ grinders**.

The idea of holidays for the workers
started in 1871 with the first bank
holidays. The arrival of the railways
meant that hard-working housemaids
and shop assistants could enjoy a day out
by the sea.

Workshop of the world

On 1 May, 1851 a new building was opened in London called the Crystal Palace. It was like a huge greenhouse and was the centrepiece of the Great **Exhibition**. The Great Exhibition was the idea of Prince Albert, Queen Victoria's husband. It was built to show off all the latest British inventions.

People came from all over the world to see it. In twenty weeks six million people visited the exhibition. It was a chance to prove to other countries that Britain was 'The Workshop of the World'. Britain's workshops – its mines, factories and shipyards – had never produced so much as they did during Victoria's reign.

Machines and inventions

Scientists and inventors from Britain, Europe and America made many important discoveries during Victoria's reign. Louis Pasteur (below) discovered an antiseptic which helped to stop infections caused by germs. Louis Daguerre invented the box-camera.

By the end of Victoria's reign rich people could listen to music on a **gramophone** and speak to a distant friend by telephone. They could ride bicycles or

even drive petrol-powered cars. They could write letters using a typewriter and then send the letters in the first 'Penny Postal' service.

The Empire

Under Queen Victoria Britain ruled the largest Empire the world had ever seen. It covered a quarter of the world's land and 400 million people lived in it. All the countries in the Empire traded with Britain. Many British people settled in the colonies, especially in Canada, New Zealand, Australia and South Africa.

Many others went abroad as soldiers, explorers and **missionaries**. They did not always treat the local people kindly but they did build railways, schools and hospitals.

Things to do

bulb holder

Make a Morse code machine

In 1838 Samuel Morse invented a code to send messages by telegraph. The code uses long (dashes) and short (dots) flashes for different letters of the alphabet.

A ·-   E ·   I ··   N -·   R ·-·   V ···-
B -···   F ··-·   J ·---   O ---   S ···   W ·--
C -·-·   G --·   K -·-   P ·--·   T -   X -··-
D -··   H ····   L ·-··   Q --·-   U ··-   Y -·--
          M --   Z --··

switch

battery

Screw a bulb into a bulb holder. Connect one side of the bulb holder to a battery. Find a small piece of wood, two drawing pins and a paperclip. Make a switch like the one in the picture. Connect the bulb holder to the switch, and the other side of the switch to the battery. When you press the paperclip down onto the drawing pin, the bulb will light up. Send a message to a friend using the Morse code.

Make a pinhole camera

Take a small cardboard box and remove the ends.

Cover one end with tissue paper and stretch it tight. Cover the other end with paper that does not let light through, or with tin foil. Make a pinhole in this piece of paper.

Point the pinhole at the window. Cover your head and everything except the front of the 'camera' with a dark cloth. You should see the window appear upside down on the back of the box.

Glossary

Blacksmiths   People who shoe horses.
Cholera   A serious disease caused by drinking dirty water.
Exhibition   A public show.
Government   The people who rule the country.
Gramophone   A record player.
Inventions   New objects that have never been made before.
Missionaries   Religious people sent to another country to make the local people believe in their religion.
Organ grinders   Street musicians who played a hand organ for money.
Threshing machine   A machine which separates the grain from the straw.
Sewers   Drains or pipes that carry away waste.
Vote   Have a say in who should govern the country.

Books to read

Growing up in Victorian England by Molly Harrison Wayland, 1980)
Everyday Life in the Nineteenth Century (Macdonald, 1983)
The Age of Machines by R. J. Unstead (Macdonald, 1974)
Charles Dickens and the Victorians by Stewart Ross (Wayland, 1986)

Index

Picture acknowledgements
Some of the illustrations in this book were originally used in *Dickens and the Victorians* in Wayland's Life and Times series.